INTROD

A Video Workshop for Infants, Children, and Adolescents contains 20 observational video segments specially selected to illustrate many of the theories, concepts, and milestones of development contained in your textbooks, *Infants and Children,* Fifth Edition and *Infants, Children, and Adolescents,* Fifth Edition, by Laura E. Berk. This guide is designed to help you make the most of this video resource, tying it to the material in the text and encouraging you to think critically about various aspects of development.

After you view a video segment (2 to 5 minutes in length), you may wish to use the corresponding questions provided to test your understanding of the material.

Although each segment of the video could lend itself to many chapters of the text, here are some suggestions:

Infants, Children, and Adolescents, **Fifth Edition**	**Suggested Video Segments**
Ch. 4: Birth and the Newborn Baby	1
Ch. 5: Physical Development in Infancy and Toddlerhood	2
Ch. 6: Cognitive Development in Infancy and Toddlerhood	1, 2, 3, 4
Ch. 7: Emotional and Social Development in Infancy and Toddlerhood	1, 3, 5
Ch. 8: Physical Development in Early Childhood	
Ch. 9: Cognitive Development in Early Childhood	6, 7, 9, 10
Ch. 10: Emotional and Social Development in Early Childhood	
Ch. 11: Physical Development in Middle Childhood	8
Ch. 12: Cognitive Development in Middle Childhood	8, 9, 10, 11
Ch. 13: Emotional and Social Development in Middle Childhood	6, 12, 13
Ch. 14: Physical Development in Adolescence	16
Ch. 15: Cognitive Development in Adolescence	14
Ch. 16: Emotional and Social Development in Adolescence	14, 15, 16, 17, 18
Ch. 17: Emerging Adulthood	19, 20

ALLYN & BACON

VideoWorkshop
A COURSE TAILORED VIDEO LEARNING SYSTEM

Student Learning Guide
with CD-ROM

for

Berk

Infants, Children, and Adolescents
Fifth Edition

and

Infants and Children
Fifth Edition

ALLYN & BACON

VideoWorkshop _____
A COURSE TAILORED VIDEO LEARNING SYSTEM

Student Learning Guide with CD-ROM

for

Berk

Infants, Children, and Adolescents
Fifth Edition

and

Infants and Children
Fifth Edition

prepared by

Laura E. Berk
Illinois State University

Sara Harris
Illinois State University

Boston   New York   San Francisco
Mexico City   Montreal   Toronto   London   Madrid   Munich   Paris
Hong Kong   Singapore   Tokyo   Cape Town   Sydney

To obtain permission(s) to use the material from this work, please submit a written request to Allyn and Bacon, Permissions Department, 75 Arlington Street, Boston, MA 02116 or fax your request to 617-848-7320.

ISBN 0-205-45745-2

Printed in the United States of America

10 9 8 7 6 5 4   09 08 07 06

CONTENTS

INFANCY AND TODDLERHOOD

PARTICIPANTS

Child	Age	To identify on video, look for...
Anna	2 weeks	White, long-sleeved shirt and diaper, white socks
Mac	3 months	Red shirt, blue overalls
Hannah	7 months	Pink bow on head, multicolored play suit with pink top
Luke	1 1/2 years	Gray shirt, black pants
Peter	2 years	Blue shirt, black pants
Sophie	2 1/2years	Purple shirt and pants
Elena	2 1/2 years	Denim jumper

Segment 1
The Newborn Baby's Capacities: Anna, 2 weeks

In this segment, 2-week-old Anna exhibits a variety of newborn reflexes and capacities. Anna's mother carefully attends to the newborn, responding to Anna's signals by speaking softly, comforting her after a diaper change, and asking if she's hungry when she begins to suck on her fingers. Next, Professor Berk holds Anna while her mother shakes a rattle, illustrating the newborn's responsiveness to sound and visual stimulation. The segment concludes with Anna demonstrating the crawling motion, moro reflex, and stepping reflex.

For Discussion

1. According to your text, some newborn reflexes provide the foundation for complex motor skills that will develop later. Does Anna demonstrate any of these reflexes? If so, which ones? How are these reflexes adaptive? Explain. (Chapter 4, pp. 148-149)

A._____

B._____

C._____

2. Using examples from the video, explain how Anna's signals evoke attention from her mother. Why is it important for caregivers to respond consistently and appropriately to infant signals? Explain. (Chapter 4, pp. 148-153; Chapter 7, pp. 269-270)

A._____

_____

_____

B._____

_____

_____

3. What term is used in your text to describe the high-pitched, exaggerated expression of Anna's mother's voice when interacting with the baby? Why is this special style of speech important? (Chapter 6, pp. 242-243)

A._____

B._____

_____

Multiple Choice Questions

1. Anna's stepping reflex
   A. suggests that she will walk sooner than most babies.
   B. will disappear once she begins walking.
   C. prepares her for voluntary walking.
   D. has no known function.

2. Pediatricians test newborn reflexes
   A. to determine when babies will reach certain motor milestones.
   B. because reflexes can reveal the health of the baby's nervous system.
   C. to help parents learn what their babies are capable of doing.
   D. to track states or arousal.

3. Which of the following statements is TRUE?
   A. Anna's visual acuity is very similar to her mother's.
   B. Anna is unable to see her mother's face.
   C. Although Anna's eye movements are slow, they are very accurate.
   D. Anna can perceive her mother's face but the image is blurry.

4. According to Bowlby, Anna is in the preattachment phase. This means
   A. built-in signals help bring Anna into close contact with her mother and other caregivers.
   B. Anna clearly prefers her mother to a stranger.
   C. Anna displays separation anxiety when her mother leaves.
   D. Anna clearly prefers Professor Berk to her mother.

5. The primary purpose of child-directed speech is to facilitate understanding and
   A. create metalinguistic awareness.
   B. maintain a child's attention.
   C. teach language to a child.
   D. teach phonemes.

Web Links

Baby Talk: Newborn Handout

This website contains a wealth of information on the newborn baby, including what to expect during the first few weeks, strategies for soothing a crying baby, and a brief description of newborn sensory capacities and reflexes.
http://www.babytalk.org/newbornhandout.html

Child Development Website

This website provides tutorials for some of the classic child development theories, such as those proposed by Freud and Erikson.
http://childstudy.net/

Tips for Getting Infants to Sleep

Prevent Child Abuse Indiana provides this information sheet for new parents, with suggestions on how to get infants to sleep through the night.
http://www.pcain.org/Services_Programs/infant_sleep.htm

Soothing a Crying Baby

This site provides suggestions for soothing a crying baby.
http://www.pregnancy-info.net/cry.html

Segment 2
Learning Capacities: Mac, 3 months

This segment opens with Mac and his father playing. The interaction between Mac and his father illustrates how fathers tend to play differently with their babies than do mothers. When presented with a rattle, Mac shows signs of voluntary reaching. Watch as Mac's mother holds up a green and then a yellow ring. He habituates to the green ring and then recovers to the yellow ring.

For Discussion

1. Why is voluntary reaching such an important developmental milestone? How does early experience affect voluntary reaching? (Chapter 5, pp. 190-191)

A._____

_____

B._____

_____

_____

2. What substage of sensorimotor development is Mac probably in? What behaviors are characteristic of this substage? What behaviors does Mac display? (Chapter 6, pp. 209-210)

A._____

B._____

_____

C._____

_____

3. According to research presented in your text, why are habituation and recovery important for learning? Explain. (Chapter 5, pp. 184-185)

_____

_____

_____

_____

Multiple Choice Questions

1. Mac's increased interest in the yellow ring after viewing the green ring is called
    A. extinction.
    B. habituation.
    C. optical flow.
    D. recovery.

5

2. Based on Mac's age, we can make the following assumption about the visual abilities that helped him perform well on the habituation/recovery task:
    A. Mac can clearly focus on the rings and distinguish their colors.
    B. Mac cannot yet distinguish green from yellow.
    C. Mac can see objects clearly only if they are 8 to 20 inches from his face, and he cannot yet see most colors.
    D. Mac's vision is now 20/20.

3. According to information-processing theorists, speed of habituation and recovery to visual stimuli are
    A. related to speed of classical conditioning.
    B. unable to tell us much about early mental progress.
    C. among the best available predictors of IQ from early childhood into adolescence.
    D. determined by scores on the Home Observation for Measurement of the Environment (HOME).

4. Research on multiple attachments indicates that
    A. babies are naturally attached to mothers but not to fathers.
    B. fathers' sensitive caregiving predicts secure attachment.
    C. quality of caregiving predicts secure infant–father attachment but does not predict secure infant–mother attachment.
    D. fathers can only develop a secure attachment with their babies if they take on a full-time child-rearing role.

5. Cross-cultural research shows that
    A. fathers' warmth contributes greatly to children's long-term favorable development.
    B. fathers' warmth only contributes to children's long-term favorable development in industrialized nations.
    C. the less time fathers spend playing with their babies, the more time they have to devote to sensitive caregiving.
    D. the relationship between mothers and fathers has little to do with the relationship between parents and their babies.

Web Links

Father Participation Links
This website provides numerous links to research and organizations dedicated to supporting father involvement in child rearing.
http://www.massey.ac.nz/~kbirks/gender/fathers.htm

Dads Can: 10 + 1 Tips to Be an Involved Father
This website presents 11 practical tips for fathers who want to become more involved in the lives of their children.
http://www.dadscan.ca/10_+_1_tips_01.html

All About Vision

This page contains information on visual development in infancy, including indications of possible vision problems.
http://www.allaboutvision.com/parents/infants.htm

Sibling Rivalry and the Birth of a New Baby

The Center for Effective Parenting tells parents what to expect from an older sibling when a new baby comes into the family. It also provides suggestions for preparing the older sibling for the arrival of the baby.
http://www.parenting-ed.org/handout3/Specific%20Concerns%20and%20
Problems/sibling%20rivalry%20&%20baby.htm

Segment 3

Object Permanence and Parent–Infant Interaction: Hannah, 7 months

This segment begins with Hannah handling two rattles. Professor Berk uses one of the rattles for several object-hiding tasks. Notice how Hannah successfully searches for the rattle when it is partially covered by a cloth diaper. However, when the rattle is completely covered, Hannah fails to search for it. Lastly, Hannah plays with her mother. As mother and baby interact, their mutual gaze and exchange of emotional signals illustrate Vygotsky's concept of intersubjectivity.

1. What does Hannah's searching behavior reveal about her understanding of object permanence? (Chapter 6, p. 211)

_____

_____

_____

_____

2. How is Hannah's mother fostering communication skills by playing peek-a-boo? Explain. (Chapter 6, p. 239)

_____

_____

_____

_____

3. Using examples from the video, describe how Hannah matches her emotional expression to that of her mother's. How does social referencing contribute to emotional development? Explain. (Chapter 7, p. 255)

A. _____

_____

_____

B. _____

_____

_____

4. Besides intersubjectivity, what other Vygotskian concepts are revealed in this segment? (Chapter 6, pp. 266-268)

_____

_____

_____

_____

5. Review the interactions between Mac and his parents. Now watch the interactions between Hannah and her mother. Do Mac's parents interact differently than Hannah's mother? That is, are their interactions gender stereotyped? (Chapter 7, pp. 262-263; Chapter 10, pp. 382-384)

_____

_____

_____

_____

_____

_____

Multiple Choice Questions

1. At one point in the video, Hannah looks behind her and her mother says, "lights." In this example, Hannah's mother is establishing
   A. child-directed speech.
   B. fast-mapping.
   C. joint attention.
   D. a gesture.

2. In uncertain situations, infants often engage in social referencing. This means they
   A. become upset around strangers.
   B. seek emotional information from a trusted person.
   C. seek emotional information from strangers.
   D. feel embarrassed or ashamed when others are watching them.

3. In the video, Hannah has difficulty finding the Kermit the Frog rattle when it is hidden under a cloth. When Professor Berk realizes that Hannah cannot find the rattle when it is completely hidden, she partially covers the rattle so Hannah can see it. Professor Berk is demonstrating the Vygotskian concept of
   A. dialectical learning.
   B. intersubjectivity.
   C. reciprocal teaching.
   D. scaffolding.

4. Hannah's ability to find the Kermit the Frog rattle when Professor Berk partially covers it shows that Hannah has some understanding of object permanence. This means Hannah
   A. understands that objects continue to exist when they are out of sight.
   B. doesn't really understand that objects continue to exist when they are out of sight.
   C. is not yet capable of mental representation.
   D. is in Piaget's preoperational stage.

5. Based on her age and research presented in your text, which of the following play materials would most likely support Hannah's cognitive development?
    A. a crib mobile
    B. picture books
    C. reading flashcards
    D. crayons and a coloring book

Web Links

Physical Knowledge in Infancy

This link provides an illustration of several violation-of-expectation problems.
http://web.uvic.ca/~lalonde/Psyc435A/object/

Stranger Anxiety

This website features a handout produced by the Center for Effective Parenting that describes seven things parents can do to minimize the anxiety the child feels during this time in his/her development.
http://www.parenting-ed.org/handout3/Specific%20Concerns%20and%20Problems/stranger%20anxiety.htm

Child Emotion Laboratory

The Child Emotion Laboratory is located in the Department of Psychology at McMaster University in Ontario, Canada. Take a virutal tour of their laboratory, find out about ongoing projects, and access recent publications.
http://www.science.mcmaster.ca/Psychology/emotionlab/child.emotion.laboratory.htm

Vygotsky Resources

This website presents a number of links on Vygotsky's life and theory. There are also resources for educators interested in applying Vygotksy's theory in the classroom.
http://www.kolar.org/vygotsky/

Supporting Early Language Learning: Luke, 1½ years, Sophie and Elena, 2½ years

This segment opens with 1 1/2-year-old Luke reading a book with his mother. Next, 2 1/2-year-old twins, Sophie and Elena, read a storybook with their mother. Notice the rich dialogue taking place between these toddlers and their mothers. Next, Sophie and Elena engage in make-believe play. Their mother comments on their activities, which helps sustain the play session and fosters language learning.

For Discussion

1. Using examples from your text and the video, explain how storybook reading facilitates language learning in infancy and toddlerhood. (Chapter 6, pp. 242-244)

_____

_____

_____

_____

2. Cite characteristics of make-believe play that Sophie and Elena demonstrate. How does the mother facilitate make-believe while also supporting the twins' language development? (Chapter 6, p. 228; 242-244)

A._____

_____

B._____

_____

_____

3. How does the referential style of language learning differ from the expressive style? Which style do Sophie and Elena seem to prefer? Use examples from the video to support your answer. (Chapter 6, pp. 241-242)

A._____

_____

B._____

_____

_____

Multiple Choice Questions

1. About the time toddlers master advanced object permanence problems, they
   A. learn to say "mommy" and "daddy."
   B. use disappearance words, such as "all gone."
   C. quit using disappearance words, such as "all gone."
   D. begin pronouncing difficult words without adult directives.

2. If Luke is like most 18-month-olds,
   A. his vocabulary consists of about 20 spoken words.
   B. he produces more words than he comprehends.
   C. he still communicates mostly by cooing and babbling.
   D. his vocabulary consists of 50 to 200 spoken words.

3. By reading to their toddlers, parents
   A. discourage their children from learning about written symbols and story structures.
   B. fail to teach their children independent reading skills.
   C. provide exposure to many aspects of language, such as vocabulary, grammar, and communication skills.
   D. support communication skills but fail to expose their children to lessons in vocabulary and grammar.

4. Conversational give-and-take between parents and toddlers
   A. is one of the best predictors of early language development and academic competence during the school years.
   B. rarely takes place during make-believe play.
   C. predicts early language development but has no impact on academic competence during the school years.
   D. should solely focus on correcting children's grammatical inconsistencies.

5. Sophie and Elena's mother frequently engages the girls in joint make-believe play. As a result, she probably
   A. treats the twins equally in other situations.
   B. encourages competition between the twins.
   C. promotes all aspects of conversational dialogue.
   D. devotes little time to storybook reading.

Web Links

Zero to Three

Zero to Three is a nonprofit organization founded in 1977 to promote the importance of healthy development for infants and toddlers from birth to 3 years of age. This site contains numerous resources for parents, educators, policymakers, and anyone interested in working with young children.
http://www.zerotothree.org/

Helping Your Child Become a Reader

The U.S. Department of Education developed this site to suggest strategies and activities for fostering literacy development from infancy through age 10.
http://www.ed.gov/parents/academic/help/reader/part3.html

Speech and Language Development

This website, sponsored by the American Speech and Hearing Association, provides numerous resources on speech and language development, including developmental milestones, age-appropriate activities for supporting language development, and information on the relationship between langauge and literacy development.
http://www.asha.org/public/speech/development/

Play and Learning in Early Childhood Classrooms

This article addresses the importance of incorporating play into early education programs.
http://www.tepsa.org/Publications/BodrovaLeong.pdf

Compliance and Self-Control: Luke, 1 1/2 years, Peter, 2 years, and Sophie and Elena, 2 1/2 years

In this segment, 1 1/2–year-old Luke and 2 1/2-year-old twins Sophie and Elena demonstrate the toddler's ability to comply with adult directives as they retrieve various objects. Next, Professor Berk presents a delay of gratification task to 2-year-old Peter and to Sophie and Elena. Notice how Peter immediately eats the M & Ms, whereas Sophie and Elena wait for Professor Berk to return before eating the candy. In a second delay of gratification task, Sophie and Elena again demonstrate self-control as they wait for Professor Berk to return before looking in a bag for presents. Notice the strategies they use to delay gratification.

For Discussion

1. Cite examples of compliance and noncompliance in these children. What can parents do to foster compliance? (Chapter 7, p. 280)

A._____
_____
_____

B._____
_____
_____

2. What self-control strategies do Sophie and Elena use during the delay of gratification tasks? Does the girls' mother use any techniques to help them as they wait for Professor Berk? Use examples from the video to support your answer. (Chapter 7, pp. 280-281)

A._____
_____
_____

B._____
_____
_____

3. Why is the development of self-control especially important in the first few years of life? (Chapter 7, p. 280)

_____
_____
_____

Multiple Choice Questions

1. The development of self-control
    A. does not truly emerge until children are 5 or 6 years old.
    B. is essential for moral development.
    C. emerges earlier in boys than in girls.
    D. emerges earlier in children from large families.

2. To behave in a self-controlled fashion, children must
    A. think of themselves as separate, autonomous beings.
    B. understand the intentions of others.
    C. have siblings who model self-controlled behavior.
    D. think of themselves as extensions of their parents.

3. When Sophie refuses to get the ball for her mother, she is
    A. demonstrating a lack of self-control.
    B. being disobedient and should be punished
    C. asserting her autonomy.
    D. probably confused by her mother's request.

4. Sophie's mother can effectively deal with her opposition by
    A. ignoring Sophie's behavior.
    B. responding in a warm manner and gently encouraging Sophie to comply with her request.
    C. forcing Sophie to do as she says.
    D. only issuing commands to Elena, who is more compliant.

5. Which of the following suggestions can parents use to help their toddlers develop compliance and self-control?
    A. Establish strict rules and make sure toddlers comply with those rules.
    B. Do nothing—compliance and self-control develop automatically.
    C. When toddlers repeatedly defy parental commands, consider using authoritarian child-rearing techniques.
    D. Respond to self-controlled behavior with verbal and physical approval.

Web Links

Teaching Young Children Self-Control Skills
The National Mental Health and Education Center has prepared a fact sheet for parents and educators to help them understand how they can help young children develop important self-control skills.
http://www.naspcenter.org/pdf/behavior%20template.pdf

What Does Your Toddler Really Know About "No?"

This newsletter provides parents with alternatives to using shame and guilt as a way of gaining compliance from their toddlers.
http://www.parenting-plus.com/newsletter_0108.htm

Toilet Training

Safer Child, Inc. provides a number of practical suggestions about toilet training for parents with young children.
http://www.saferchild.com/potty.htm

Child and Family Canada

Search this Canadian public education website for information on child care, policies for family and work, online articles, and other resources pertaining to child development, education, and parenting.
http://www.cfc-efc.ca/

EARLY CHILDHOOD

PARTICIPANTS

Child	Age	To identify on video, look for...
Sophie	2 years, 3 months	Plaid shirt, pink sweater, blue pants
Alison	4 years	Blond hair, green dress

Segment 6

Enhancing Make-Believe Play in Early Childhood: Sophie, 2 years 3 months

In this segment, Sophie's father creates a zone of proximal development by guiding and supporting her make-believe. As they interact, he offers suggestions, asks questions, and responds to her actions and verbalizations. In doing so, he fosters Sophie's cognitive and language development.

For Discussion

1. In what ways are Piaget and Vygotsky's views of make-believe play similar? How are they different? (Chapter 9, pp. 316-318; 330-331)

A._____

_____

_____

B._____

_____

_____

2. Using examples from the video, explain how her father's participation helps Sophie create more elaborate play themes than if she were left to play by herself. Why is adult participation so crucial? (Chapter 9, p. 330)

A._____

_____

_____

_____

B._____

_____

_____

3. Vygotsky believed that make-believe play leads development forward in two ways. The first is mentioned above, in the summary. What is the second way? (Chapter 6, p. 228)

_____

_____

_____

_____

Multiple Choice Questions

1. According to recent research, Piaget's view of make-believe play as mere practice of representational schemes is regarded as
      A. accurate for all children.
      B. accurate for children growing up in low-SES homes.
      C. too limited.
      D. more accurate than Vygotsky's view of make-believe.

2. According to Vygotsky, Sophie's father keeps the make-believe session within her _____ by asking questions, prompting, and making suggestions.
      A. zone of proximal development
      B. guided participation zone
      C. egocentric zone
      D. dual representation zone

3. When Sophie's father suggests that she use a wand to represent a lollipop, he is helping her grasp the concept of _____.
      A. animistic thinking
      B. hierarchical classification
      C. centration
      D. dual representation

4. According to Vygotsky, private speech during make-believe is important because it
      A. helps children bring action under the control of thought.
      B. helps children further develop their language skills.
      C. lets adults know what children are thinking.
      D. helps children become less egocentric.

5. Which of the following statements reflects the preschool child's growing symbolic mastery?
      A. Preschoolers rely heavily on adult input during their make-believe play.
      B. Preschoolers stumble upon themes as they experiment with make-believe play.
      C. Over time, play increasingly detaches from the real-life conditions associated with it.
      D. Make-believe play does not contribute to symbolic mastery during the preschool years.

Web Links

Helping Children with Autism Learn
>This link contains a book excerpt about the importance of play for children with autism.
>http://www.selfgrowth.com/articles/Siegel3.html

Creative Dramatics
>This website provides an overview of make-believe play, including its benefits and relevance in early childhood programs.
>http://www.jellybeanscd.com/benefits.shtml

NAEYC Accreditation: Signs of Quality in Early Childhood Programs
>This website provides information on identifying high-quality child care.
>http://www.naeyc.org/accreditation/

Childcare In Sweden
>This website provides information on childcare in Sweden.
>http://www.sweden.se/templates/FactSheet____4132.asp

Segment 7
Piagetian Tasks: Alison, 4 years

In this segment, Professor Berk presents Alison with three conservation tasks. In conservation of liquid, Alison affirms that two glasses contain equal amounts of water. But when Professor Berk pours the water from one glass into the bowl, Alison does not conserve. In conservation of number, Alison recognizes that there are equal numbers of red and white chips when they are lined up in one-to-one correspondence. However, when Professor Berk and Alison create a circle of chips, Alison indicates that the row of white chips contains more because it is a line. Next, Professor Berk repeats the task but uses only 3 red chips and 3 white chips. After the transformation, Alison determines that both arrangements have equal numbers of chips. In the final task, conservation of length, Professor Berk presents Alison with two roads. When the straws are side by side, Alison tells Professor Berk that two animals walking down the roads would have to walk the same distance. But when one straw is moved, Alison states that the lengths of the roads are not longer equal.

For Discussion

1. What does Alison's performance on the conservation tasks reveal about her thinking? Is her performance consistent with Piaget's description of the preoperational child? Explain. (Chapter 9, pp. 319-321)

A._____

_____

_____

_____

_____

B._____

_____

_____

_____

2. In the first conservation of number problem, Alison told Professor Berk that there were more white chips than red chips after the red chips had been placed in a circle. But when Professor Berk repeated the problem with fewer chips, Alison correctly solved the problem. Why was Alison successful the second time but not the first? (Chapter 9, pp. 320-321)

_____

_____

_____

_____

_____

3. Based on her performance on the conservation tasks, how would you expect Alison to perform on a Piagetian class inclusion problem? Explain. (Chapter 9, pp. 320-321)

_____
_____
_____
_____

4. Referring to your text, what does recent research reveal about the preoperational child? Was Piaget correct to assume that the preschooler is cognitively deficient? Explain. (Chapter 9, pp. 326-327)

A._____
_____
_____

B._____
_____
_____

Multiple Choice Questions

1. According to Piaget, one reason preoperational children have difficulty with conservation is that their understanding is characterized by centration. This means they
    A. are unable to mentally go through a series of steps in a problem and reverse direction.
    B. focus on one aspect of a situation, neglecting other important features.
    C. believe inanimate objects have lifelike qualities.
    D. fail to distinguish the symbolic viewpoints of others from their own viewpoint.

2. Suppose Alison tells you she has one brother and no sisters. If you ask her if her brother has any sisters, she tells you no. What cognitive limitation is Alison demonstrating?
    A. animistic thinking
    B. centration
    C. exclusion
    D. irreversibility

3. Recent research on Piaget's three mountains problem suggests that
    A. 4-year-olds can correctly solve the problem if more familiar objects are used.
    B. Piaget was correct about the egocentric preschooler.
    C. preoperational children cannot solve the problem because their depth perception is not fully developed.
    D. most preoperational children correctly solve the problem if given the time.

4. When Professor Berk simplifies one of the conservation tasks and presents it to Alison, she
     A. is still unable to solve the task.
     B. becomes frustrated and gives up.
     C. correctly solves the task.
     D. tells Professor Berk that she's ready to play another game.

5. Which of the following statements illustrates Piaget's contribution to early childhood education?
     A. Piagetian teachers should focus on speeding up development.
     B. To ensure that all children learn at the same rate, Piagetian teachers should plan the same activities for all students.
     C. Piagetian teachers should emphasize one activity at a time so children don't become confused.
     D. Piagetian teachers should provide a rich variety of activities to promote exploration and discovery.

Web Links

The Jean Piaget Society
The Jean Piaget Society was established in 1970 to provide a forum for the study of cognitive development. At this site, you will find a biography of Piaget and can learn about upcoming conferences based on his work and ideas.
http://www.piaget.org/

National Library of Virtual Manipulatives
This website contains an interactive simulation of Piaget's conservation of liquid problem. At the homepage, type Piaget into the search box. Then select one of the activities next to How High?
http://matti.usu.edu/nlvm/nav/index.html

Constructivist Learning Design
This link provides information on applying constructivist learning theory (discovery learning) in the classroom.
http://www.prainbow.com/cld/cldn.html

Early Childhood Education Center
This website provides an overview of a Piagetian preschool program sponsored by the Department of Psychology at the University of Waterloo.
http://watarts.uwaterloo.ca/psychology/ecec/

MIDDLE CHILDHOOD

PARTICIPANTS

Child	Age	To identify on video, look for...
Logan	4 years	Blue dress with black collar
Nicole	5 years	Blue shirt, blue headband
Zoe	7 years	Light blue T-shirt
Kerry	7 years	Blue sweatshirt with flowers
Victor	7 years	Red short-sleeved T-shirt

Segment 8
The Children's Circus

This segment illustrates how the physical changes of middle childhood contribute to dramatic motor accomplishment, as students participate in the Children's Circus at Metcalf School, Illinois State University. Watch as students walk tight ropes, assist one another on balance beams, and tumble on mats set up in the gym.

For Discussion

1. What gross motor skills of middle childhood are demonstrated in this video? What physical changes contribute to these new and improved skills? (Chapter 11, pp. 417-418)

A._____

_____

_____

_____

B._____

_____

_____

_____

2. Using examples from the video, explain how the Children's Circus appeals to and supports individual differences in motor capacities. Are sex differences in athletic ability evident? At about what age do they appear, and what biological and environmental factors might contribute to these differences? (Chapter 11, pp. 418-419)

A._____

_____

_____

_____

B._____

_____

C._____

_____

_____

_____

3. How is cooperative learning and multigrade grouping used in the Children's Circus? What are the benefits of these practices in schools? (Chapter 12, pp. 456-459)

A._____

_____

_____

_____

B._____

_____

4. What are some benefits of including health and physical education in schools? Include not only the physical benefits but also the social and cognitive benefits associated with regular exercise and knowledge of health and illness. (Chapter 11, pp. 414-416)

Physical: _____

_____

_____

_____

Social: _____

_____

_____

Cognitive: _____

_____

_____

_____

5. How might regular exercise and knowledge of health and illness in middle childhood contribute to psychological well-being during puberty? How can this knowledge help protect adolescents from developing eating disorders, engaging in risky sexual activity, and experimenting with drugs and alcohol? (Chapter 11, pp. 414-416; Chapter 14, pp. 525-526; 532-538)

A._____

_____

_____

B._____

_____

_____

_____

_____

_____

_____

Multiple Choice Questions

1. Most efforts to impart health information to school-age children
   A. have little impact on behavior.
   B. are very effective.
   C. cause anxiety and fear.
   D. only work for children who are concerned about their physical appearance.

2. The gross motor achievements of middle childhood reflect gains in
   A. running and throwing.
   B. flexibility, balance, agility, and force.
   C. flexibility, running, and strength.
   D. size and strength.

3. Both boys and girls perform similarly in the Children's Circus. This suggests that
   A. the tasks are physically unchallenging.
   B. the girls are much stronger than the boys.
   C. the boys weren't trying very hard.
   D. the physical capacities of school-age boys and girls are similar.

4. Regarding athletic performance, parents
   A. have little influence on their children's performance.
   B. tend to have high expectations for both sons and daughters.
   C. tend to perceive their daughters as athletically skilled but are unaware of ways to support their talent.
   D. hold higher expectations for boys' performance.

5. To promote physical activity in middle childhood, schools should
     A. emphasize training in competitive sports.
     B. require only weekly physical education classes so children won't feel overwhelmed by the extra activity.
     C. emphasize informal games that most children can perform well.
     D. separate boys and girls.

Web Links

Department of Health

This website is sponsored by the United Kingdom's Department of Health. You will find a wealth of information on child and adolescent health care and public policies.
http://www.dh.gov.uk/Home/fs/en

Public Health Agency of Canada

Designed to bring national attention to the health and well being of Canadian children and adolescents, this website provides information on public policies, education, early intervention programs, longitudinal research, and upcoming projects.
http://www.phac-aspc.gc.ca/dca-dea/main_e.html

Bright Futures in Practice: Physical Activity

This website, sponsored by Georgetown University, provides information about the importance of physical activity for healthy development in children and adolescents.
http://www.brightfutures.org/physicalactivity/

Children's Safety Network

Sponsored by the U.S. Department of Health and Human Services and the Maternal and Child Health Bureau, the Children's Safety Network (CSN) provides information to health agencies and other organizations interested in reducing unintentional injuries in and violence toward children.
http://www.childrenssafetynetwork.org/

Segment 9
Class Inclusion Task: Nicole, 5 years and Zoe, 7 years

In this segment, Professor Berk presents a class inclusion problem to 5-year-old Nicole and 7-year-old Zoe. Whereas Nicole is unable to solve the problem, Zoe easily reasons hierarchically, illustrating the more logical, flexible, and organized thought that develops in middle childhood.

For Discussion

1. Using examples from her response to Professor Berk, what errors did Nicole make when she tried to solve the problem? How might Professor Berk have altered the task to help Nicole solve it? (Chapter 9, pp. 321, 323)

A._____

_____

B._____

_____

_____

_____

2. Cite cognitive advances that permit older children like Zoe to successfully solve this problem. (Chapter 12, p. 428)

_____

_____

_____

_____

3. Besides gains in cognition, what environmental factors contribute to the school-age child's ability to solve Piagetian tasks? (Chapter 12, p. 430)

_____

_____

_____

Multiple Choice Questions

1. To solve Piaget's class inclusion problem, Zoe had to
   A. become egocentric.
   B. focus on three relations at once.
   C. show an awareness of spatial reasoning.
   D. seriate mentally.

33

2. Which of the following limitations explains why Nicole was unable to solve the class inclusion task?
> A. animistic thinking
> B. inability to conserve
> C. difficulty noticing transformations
> D. lack of hierarchical classification

3. School-age children's improved ability to classify is evident in their
> A. make-believe play.
> B. focus on games without rules.
> C. interest in collecting items, such as stamps, coins, and baseball cards.
> D. improved reaction time during physical activities.

4. Research indicates that
> A. cultural and school practices contribute to mastery of Piagetian tasks.
> B. cultural and school practices have no impact on mastery of Piagetian tasks.
> C. cultural practices influence mastery of Piagetian tasks only in industrialized nations.
> D. children in all cultures perform equally well on Piagetian tasks.

5. Some neo-Piagetian theorists argue that the development of operational thinking can best be understood in terms of
> A. a discontinuous restructuring of children's thinking.
> B. educational background.
> C. gains in information-processing capacity.
> D. a sudden shift to a new stage.

Web Links

Piaget's Concrete Operational Stage
> This site provides information on Piaget's concrete operational stage, including suggestions for teaching children during this period of development.
> http://www.columbiastate.edu/matlock/concrete_operational_hout.htm

Teachers of Middle Childhood
> Sponsored by the Indiana Professional Standards Board, this website provides standards for teaching school-age children.
> http://www.in.gov/psb/standards/MiddleChildDevStds.html

Learning Strategies Database
> The Center for Advancement of Learning provides information on the contributions of information-processing theory to the understanding of children's learning strategies.
> http://www.muskingum.edu/~cal/database/memory.html

Health Central: Memory Quiz
This link takes you to a free short-term memory test developed by the
Memory Assessment Clinic of Bethesda, Maryland.
http://www.healthcentral.com/cooltools/CT_mentalhealth/CT_memory_quiz.cfm

Segment 10
False Belief: Logan, 4 years and Zoe, 7 years

In this segment, Professor Berk presents a false-belief task to 4-year-old Logan and 7-year-old Zoe. First, the girls are shown two boxes, one a Band-Aid box and the other a box covered with colored paper. When asked to select the box with the Band-Aids, they discover that the marked box is empty while the unmarked box actually holds the Band-Aids. Then the girls are asked to predict where a naïve puppet might look for some Band-Aids. Notice how Logan erroneously selects the marked box, whereas Zoe selects the unmarked box. The segment ends with Professor Berk presenting a second-order false belief task to Zoe, in which she must explain how one character's beliefs about a situation differ from a second character's beliefs.

For Discussion

1. How does Logan's understanding of the mind differ from Zoe's? What factors contribute to the young child's understanding of mental life? How about the school-age child? (Chapter 9, pp. 336-337; Chapter 12, p. 437)

A._____

_____

_____

B._____

_____

_____

2. How can parents and teachers help foster the development of false belief? Can you think of ways in which scaffolding and the zone of proximal development might be applicable? (Chapter 6, p. 227; Chapter 9, p. 330; 337-338)

A._____

_____

_____

B._____

_____

_____

3. How does school-age children's improved ability to reflect on their own mental life contribute to advances in problem solving? (Chapter 12, p. 437)

_____

_____

_____

Multiple Choice Questions

1. Which of the following factors have likely contributed to Logan's understanding of the mind?
   - A. autobiographical memory
   - B. scripts
   - C. language and cognitive skills
   - D. ordinality

2. Which of the following is TRUE about the young child's theory of mind?
   - A. Preschoolers have virtually no awareness of mental activities.
   - B. Preschoolers usually conclude that mental activity stops when there are no obvious cues to indicate that a person is thinking.
   - C. Preschoolers do not understand that thinking takes place inside their heads.
   - D. Preschoolers do not understand that people behave in ways consistent with desires.

3. School-age children like Zoe view the mind as a(n)
   - A. passive container of information.
   - B. type of memory strategy.
   - C. confusing mass of information.
   - D. active, constructive agent.

4. By age 7, children are aware that
   - A. second-order beliefs can be wrong.
   - B. second-order beliefs are always right.
   - C. beliefs but not desires influence behavior.
   - D. desires but not beliefs influence behavior.

5. Which of the following statements about Logan and Zoe is TRUE?
   - A. Both Logan and Zoe have a similar understanding of the mind.
   - B. Logan is far more conscious of memory strategies than is Zoe.
   - C. Zoe is far more conscious of memory strategies than is Logan.
   - D. If Professor Berk presented the second-order false-belief task to Logan, she would likely perform similarly to Zoe.

Web Links

Theory of Mind

This link provides a number of resources that address the topic of autism and theory of mind.

http://groups.msn.com/TheAutismHomePage/theoryofmind.msnw

False Belief

This article examines false-belief performance in Mayan children.
http://www.sci-con.org/articles/20040501.html

Children's Understanding of What is "Real" on Television

This article explores the relationship between children's cognitive development and their understanding of television.
http://www.aber.ac.uk/media/Documents/short/realrev.html

Visual Media and Young Children's Attention Span

In this article, written by Gloria DeGaetano, a well-known expert on children and media and the author of *Screen Smarts: A Family Guide to Media Literacy,* considers the effect of television viewing on children's attention spans.
http://users.stargate.net/~cokids/VisualMedia.html

Segment 11
A Second-Grade Math Lesson

This segment features a group of second-grade students, whose teacher has them apply their math knowledge to a real-life situation—shopping at a rain forest store. Watch as the children actively participate in the lesson by selecting items to buy, determining how much money is required to purchase those items, and explaining how they arrived at their answers. Also, notice how the math lesson is rich in dialogue. The teacher not only guides the activity but encourages students to comment on and discuss one another's purchases.

For Discussion

1. What type of classroom, traditional or constructivist, is being depicted in this segment? What are some characteristics of this type of classroom? According to research presented in your text, what are some advantages of this type of classroom? (Chapter 12, pp. 455-456)

A._____

B._____

_____

_____

C._____

_____

_____

2. Cite instances of private speech in this video clip. Why is private speech important for cognitive development? (Chapter 9, p. 329)

_____

_____

_____

_____

_____

_____

3. Watch as the children participate in the math lesson. What strategies are being used? Why is experimentation with multiple strategies important for learning? Explain. (Chapter 12, pp. 433-436)

A._____

_____

_____

_____

B._____

_____

_____

_____

Multiple Choice Questions

1. In a traditional classroom,
    A. the teacher encourages children to take responsibility for rule making and many of the classroom activities.
    B. children work in groups for most of the day.
    C. the teacher is the sole authority for knowledge, rules, and decision making.
    D. students are evaluated by considering their progress in relation to their own prior development.

2. Which of the following choices is the best example of a constructivist classroom?
    A. Students sit at their desks and listen to the teacher explain today's lesson.
    B. Students watch a video on ocean life and then answer the teacher's questions.
    C. To learn about the rain forest, students move in pairs around the room at their own pace, stopping at different work stations where they must solve problems together.
    D. Students in a math class work on problems at their desk and then nominate a peer to write the solutions on the board.

3. What role does class size play in student learning?
    A. Class size is irrelevant as long as the teacher is experienced.
    B. In small classes, students have less work so they perform better.
    C. Larger classes are better because students have more opportunities to interact with one another.
    D. A small class size allows students to receive more individual attention from the teacher, which enhances learning.

4. In _____ classrooms, academic achievement, self-esteem, and attitudes toward school are more favorable.
    A. multigrade
    B. homogenous
    C. traditional
    D. large

5. Regarding mathematics instruction,
    A. research shows that drill and repetition help children master problem-solving skills more quickly than do other methods.
    B. encouraging children to apply strategies and making sure they understand why certain ones work are vital for solid mastery of basic math.
    C. in Asian classrooms, much more time is spent on drill and repetition than on exploring math concepts.
    D. school-age children prefer learning through drill and repetition.

Web Links

Trends in International Mathematics and Science Study (TIMMS)

This site contains a wealth of research and information on international mathematics and science instruction.
http://nces.ed.gov/timss/

Cooperative Learning Elementary Activities

This website provides a number of cooperative learning activities for school-age children. A good resource for teachers or anyone interested in curriculum design and instruction.
http://204.184.214.251/coop/ecoopmain.html

Cognitively Guided Instruction: Mathematics for Parents

Developed by the University of Wisconsin, this link provides access to a series of pamphlets to help parents support their children's understanding of mathematical concepts.
http://www.wcer.wisc.edu/MIMS/Parent_Newsletters/

The Jigsaw Classroom

This site provides information on a unique cooperative learning technique designed to promote learning and motivation and reduce racial conflict in school-age children.
http://www.jigsaw.org/

Segment 12
Moral Reasoning: Zoe, 7 years

Seven-year-old Zoe is presented with several scenarios in which she must reason about distributive justice, moral rules, social conventions, and matters of personal choice. As Professor Berk questions Zoe, notice the reasoning she uses to justify her answers.

For Discussion

1. Based on her responses, what factors does Zoe take into account when judging the actions of others? How do those factors contribute to the school-age child's ability to reason about moral rules and social conventions? (Chapter 13, p. 483)

A._____

_____

_____

B._____

_____

_____

2. In her discussion of Suzie's choice of crackers at snack time, what does Zoe's answer reveal about her understanding of matters of personal choice? How does this understanding contribute to gains in moral development? (Chapter 13, p. 483)

A._____

_____

_____

B._____

_____

_____

3. Using Damon's sequence and examples from the video, explain what level of distributive justice reasoning Zoe demonstrates. How does advanced distributive justice reasoning contribute to positive peer relations? (Chapter 13, p. 481; 485-488)

A._____

_____

_____

B._____

_____

_____

4. Review the four styles of child rearing discussed on pages 388-389 of your text. How might each style of parenting contribute to the school-age child's reasoning about distributive justice, moral rules, social conventions, and matters of personal choice? (Chapter 13, pp. 481-482)

_____
_____
_____
_____
_____
_____
_____
_____
_____
_____

5. According to your text, what are some of the pros and cons of providing moral education in public schools? What is your opinion on this topic, and why? (Chapter 14, p. 484)

_____
_____
_____
_____
_____
_____
_____
_____
_____
_____

Multiple Choice Questions

1. According to Damon,
   A. peer interactions have little influence on children's developing ideas of justice.
   B. children younger than age 10 have a very primitive understanding of distributive
      justice.
   C. the give-and-take of peer interaction supports children's developing ideas of
      justice.
   D. school-age children rarely engage in sharing without adult prompts.

2. Zoe understands that special consideration should be given to those at a disadvantage. According to Damon, Zoe is demonstrating an understanding of
   A. equality.
   B. merit.
   C. benevolence.
   D. undifferentiated perspective taking.

3. Which of the following contributes to gains in moral understanding during middle childhood?
      A. an expanding social world and gains in perspective taking
      B. strict parental instruction
      C. the ability to understand false beliefs
      D. media images and classroom instruction

4. As early as age 6, children
      A. engage in third-party perspective taking.
      B. view freedom of speech and religion as individual rights.
      C. regard social conventions with a clear purpose as very similar to social conventions with no obvious justification.
      D. engage in societal perspective taking.

5. Regarding moral education,
      A. there is little debate about what components of morality should be taught in public schools.
      B. Narvaez suggests teaching only two moral components: moral sensitivity and moral motivation.
      C. most programs are broadly focused.
      D. debate over whether and how to teach morality in the public schools is vigorous.

Web Links

Educators for Social Responsibility
      This website contains articles, resources, and curriculum materials designed for promoting social responsibility schools.
      http://www.esrnational.org/home.htm

Association for Moral Education
      This website provides information about combining moral theory with educational practices.
      http://www.amenetwork.org/

Play and the School-Age Child
      This fact sheet examines how play contributes to understanding of morality, including suggestions for fostering moral development in children.
      http://www.umext.maine.edu/onlinepubs/htmpubs/famissues/8048.htm

Parent Toolbox: Moral Development of Children
      This link presents suggestions and resources for parents who want to support moral development in their children.
      http://www.fathersworld.com/fatherhood/article.cfm?template=parenttool&article_id=219

Segment 13
Friendship: Second Graders

In this segment, second graders discuss friendship with their teacher. When asked to provide some rules for being a good friend, students mention acts of kindness, such as sharing and comforting someone who is unhappy. Next, Victor and Kerry describe one of their good friends. Notice how they emphasize personal qualities in their descriptions. For example, Victor describes his friend as kind, generous, and smart, while Kerry explains that her friend has no pets, likes flowers, and helps her when she needs it.

For Discussion

1. This segment opens with the teacher asking students to give some rules for being a good friend. How do friendships during the school years differ from friendships formed in preschool? (Chapter 10, p. 368; Chapter 13, p. 486)

_____
_____
_____
_____

2. Using research to support your answer, explain how advances in perspective taking contribute to children's understanding of friendship. (Chapter 13, pp. 480, 486)

_____
_____
_____
_____
_____
_____

3. According to your text, how do friendships between boys and girls differ? Are sex differences in friendship evident in this segment? Explain. (Chapter 13, p. 480)

A._____
_____

B._____
_____
_____

Multiple Choice Questions

1. Compared to friendships in early childhood, school-age children's friendships are
    - A. less selective.
    - B. more selective.
    - C. simply a matter of engaging in the same activities.
    - D. characterized by jealousy and conflict.

2. Children tend to select friends who are
    - A. of the other sex.
    - B. similar in age but different in ethnicity and SES.
    - C. like themselves in age, sex, race, ethnicity, and SES.
    - D. of a higher-SES background.

3. Which of the following would Victor and Kerry likely regard as serious breaches of friendship?
    - A. having more than one "best friend"
    - B. having friends with different interests
    - C. having friends from a different school
    - D. breaking promises

4. Which of the following statements is TRUE?
    - A. Friendships often dissolve when disputes arise.
    - B. Close friendships have a negative impact on peer acceptance.
    - C. Friendship provides an important context in which children learn to tolerate criticism and resolve disputes.
    - D. School and neighborhood characteristics have little impact on friendship choices.

5. Compared to Victor, Kerry probably
    - A. probably demands greater closeness with her friends.
    - B. probably feels less close to her friends.
    - C. is more likely to be rejected by her peers.
    - D. is more likely to be socially awkward with her friends.

Web Links

Peer Influence

This link contains information about the influence of peers and tips for parents on how to support children's peer relations and friendships.
http://www.sylviarimm.com/peers.htm

Perspective Taking

On this website created by Ripple Effects, you will find scenarios and discussion questions on a variety of topics related to emotions and emotional self-regulation. Topics include: perspective taking, fear, grief, guilt, and identifying with others.
http://www.rippleeffects.com/resist/teens/perspective/scenario.html

Children Without Friends

This website presents a four-part article on children without friends, including problems encountered by rejected children, reasons for peer rejection, and ways to improve social skills.
http://www.nncc.org/Guidance/dc26_wo.friends1.html

Anti-Bullying Network

This website, developed by the University of Edinburgh in Scotland, presents information about bullying, including how parents, teachers, and students can tackle this problem.
http://www.antibullying.net/

ADOLESCENCE

PARTICIPANTS

Child	Age	To identify on video, look for...
Ryan	11 years	White shirt with black collar
Carmen	12 years	White shirt under gray sweatshirt
Eric	12 years	Blue and gray sweater
High School Seniors	17 years	Five young people
Mari	13 years	Blond hair, light green shirt, white pants
Sarah	13 years	Black hair, black jacket and pants
Lisa	15 years	Olive green shirt
Haley	17 years	White dress shirt
Mike	18 years	Blue sweatshirt

Segment 14
A High School History Class

In this segment, high school students discuss the Protestant Reformation that took place in Europe in the sixteenth century. Martin Luther was a key figure in the Reformation and believed the Catholic Church to be corrupt. He was upset that the Church sold extravagant pieces of art with the promise of forgiveness of sins and decreased time in purgatory. Luther published a list of grievances against the Church called *The Ninety-Five Theses*. In the list, Luther harshly criticized the church's conduct and demanded reform. His actions eventually led to a split in the Catholic Church. Watch as students discuss Martin Luther and the Reformation. They express their own viewpoints and debate with one another in a structured manner.

For Discussion

1. Numerous examples of critical and abstract thinking are evident in this video clip. List some of these examples. How does critical and abstract thinking contribute to adolescent identity formation? Explain. (Chapter 15, pp. 552-553; 560).

A._____

_____

_____

_____

B._____

_____

_____

2. In this segment, students are seated in a circle and are free to voice their opinions without being called on by the teacher. However, the teacher does facilitate discussion by asking questions. Why is this type of open forum beneficial for students? (Chapter 15, pp. 569 570)

_____

_____

_____

_____

_____

_____

_____

3. How is the discussion of Martin Luther and the Reformation a type of moral dilemma? What experiences might have contributed to these students' moral reasoning? (Chapter 16, pp. 595-600)

A._____

_____

B._____

_____

_____

_____

_____

Multiple Choice Questions

1. According to Piaget, two major features of the formal operational stage are
    A. puberty and identity development.
    B. abstract thinking and identity development.
    C. argumentativeness and self-focusing.
    D. hypothetico-deductive reasoning and prepositional thought.

2. Research on Piaget's formal operational stage indicates that
    A. most adolescents are capable of solving formal operational tasks.
    B. less than 10 percent of adults can solve formal operational tasks.
    C. about 40 to 60 percent of college students fail formal operational tasks.
    D. it emerges at the same time in most cultures.

3. In their discussion of Martin Luther and the Protestant Reformation, adolescents display idealism and criticism. According to your text, these features of cognition are
    A. related to unhealthy identity development.
    B. advantageous since they help adolescents learn how to win arguments.
    C. advantageous because they allow adolescents to work constructively for social change.
    D. signs of immaturity.

4. Which of the following suggestions can help parents handle teenagers' new capacity for abstract thought?
    A. Refrain from deciding for the adolescent.
    B. Always make decisions for adolescents since they often make poor choices.
    C. Ignore or joke with adolescents about their exaggerated sense of personal uniqueness.
    D. When adolescents become argumentative or critical, implement some sort of punishment or consequence.

5. Research supports Piaget's belief that
    A. adolescents are egocentric.
    B. interaction among peers who confront one another with differing viewpoints promotes moral understanding.
    C. moral reasoning rarely guides behavior.
    D. adolescents have difficulty reasoning with peers about moral dilemmas.

Web Links

Inside the Teenage Brain

This website presents excerpts from a PBS series examining adolescent behavior using research on brain development.

http://www.pbs.org/wgbh/pages/frontline/shows/teenbrain/

Kohlberg Dilemmas

This website presents four moral dilemmas and a series of questions typically used to evaluate moral reasoning.

http://www.haverford.edu/psych/ddavis/p109g/kohlberg.dilemmas.html

Adolescent Decision Making

Presented by the National Research Council, this site examines adolescent decision-making, including implications for youth programs.

http://www.nap.edu/html/adolescent/#framework

A Checklist for an Effective Parent-School Partnership

Sponsored by the National Campaign for Public School Improvement, this site presents a best practices approach to creating parent–school partnerships.

http://www.projectappleseed.org/chklst.html

Segment 15
Changes in Self-Concept from Middle Childhood to Adolescence: Zoe, 7 years, Eric, 12 years, Carmen, 12 years, and Lisa, 15 years

In this segment, 7-year-old Zoe, 12-year-old Eric, 12-year-old Carmen, and 15-year-old Lisa are asked to describe themselves. Notice how Zoe focuses more on concrete characteristics, whereas Eric, Carmen, and Lisa include personality traits, competencies, and social virtues.

For Discussion

1. What types of social experiences have likely contributed to the self-concepts of Eric, Carmen, and Lisa? (Chapter 16, p. 589)

_____

_____

_____

2. What factors are responsible for revisions in self-concept during middle childhood and adolescence? (Chapter 13, pp. 471-472; Chapter 16, pp. 587-588)

_____

_____

_____

3. How does self-concept contribute to peer relations in adolescence? (Chapter 16, pp. 587-588, 607)

_____

_____

_____

Multiple Choice Questions

1. In middle childhood, children's self-concepts emphasize
    A. specific behaviors.
    B. competencies.
    C. family values.
    D. social status.

2. The changing content of the school-age child's self-concept is
    A. solely the product of cognitive capacities.
    B. no longer influenced by feedback from others.
    C. a product of both cognitive capacities and feedback from others.
    D. primarily focused on personality traits.

3. As early adolescents' social world expands,
   A. contradictory self-descriptions increase.
   B. contradictory self-descriptions decrease.
   C. generalizations about the self become increasingly negative.
   D. self-descriptions become increasingly fragmented.

4. On the basis of research presented in the text, which of the following statements about Eric, Carmen, and Lisa is TRUE?
   A. Their self-concepts are very similar to children Zoe's age.
   B. Their self-esteem is on the decline.
   C. They are mostly unconcerned about others' opinions.
   D. Their self-esteem is on the rise.

5. _____ parenting predicts stable, favorable self-esteem in adolescence.
   A. Authoritarian
   B. Permissive
   C. Authoritative
   D. Uninvolved

Web Links

Self-Esteem Test
   This site provides a free self-esteem quiz, which takes about 10 minutes to complete.
   http://www.testcafe.com/sest/?affil=

About Face
   About Face is an organization devoted to promoting self-esteem in girls and women. At this website, you can find numerous resources and educational materials.
   http://www.about-face.org/

Building Self-Esteem
   This page provides a brief summary of the importance of positive self-esteem and lists a number of resources related to the topic.
   http://www.keepkidshealthy.com/adolescent/adolescentquicktips/selfesteem.html

National Association for Self-Esteem
   This website provides a number of articles and resources on self-esteem, including its relationship to school achievement, crime and violence, teenage pregnancy, and high school dropout.
   http://www.self-esteem-nase.org/research.shtml

Segment 16
Identity and Relationships with Parents: High School Seniors

This segment features a group of high school seniors discussing their identity development and the role of parents in this process. Notice how the students credit their parents with their early sense of self. However, the students point out that their views are now considerably different from those of their parents. They mention peers, the desire to be a unique individual, and exploration of others' viewpoints as important influences on their current identity.

For Discussion

1. According to Erikson, the psychological conflict of adolescence is called identity versus identity confusion. What does this mean? Are there examples of this conflict in the video clip? Explain. (Chapter 16, p. 586)

A._____

_____

_____

B._____

_____

_____

_____

2. How does adolescent physical growth contribute to identity development? (Chapter 14, pp. 517-519; 525-526; Chapter 16, p. 591)

_____

_____

_____

_____

_____

3. Using research to support your answer, explain how parents can help adolescents develop a healthy identity. (Chapter 16, p. 591)

A._____

_____

_____

_____

B._____

_____

4. Return to Chapter 1 of your text and review ecological systems theory (pp. 27-29). How do various levels of the environment contribute to adolescent identity development? (Chapter 16, pp. 591-592)

_____
_____
_____
_____
_____
_____
_____
_____

Multiple Choice Questions

1. What role do self-concept and self-esteem play in adolescent identity development?
    A. They provide the foundation for forming an identity.
    B. They have no role in identity development.
    C. Adolescents with positive self-descriptions and high self-esteem often end up diffused.
    D. Adolescents with negative self-descriptions and low self-esteem are often more motivated than their peers to become identity achieved.

2. Research indicates that
    A. adolescents who get stuck in moratorium usually become maladjusted adults.
    B. persistently diffused teenagers move toward achievement as long as their parents give them time to explore their options.
    C. identity achievement and moratorium are psychologically healthy routes to a mature self-definition.
    D. long-term foreclosure and diffusion are psychologically healthy routes to a mature self-definition.

3. In the video, several people mention peers as an important influence on identity. According to your text, peers
    A. actually have little influence on identity development.
    B. have a much greater influence on identity development than parents.
    C. often have a negative impact on identity development.
    D. expose adolescents to new ideas and values, which contribute to identity development.

4. Which of the following suggestions supports healthy identity development?
    A. Insist that children and teenagers associate primarily with popular peers.
    B. Discourage young people from exploring their ethnic heritage since this can cause confusion over who is "the real me."
    C. Initiate discussions that promote high-level thinking at home and school.
    D. Use authoritarian parenting to keep young people away from peers, who may have different values than their family.

5. Which is the single most consistent predictor of mental health in adolescence?
    A. peer relationships
    B. quality of parent-child relationships
    C. academic achievement
    D. SES

Web Links

Parenting Adolescents
This link provides information for both parents and adolescents on how to understand the teenage years.
http://www.parentingadolescents.com/

Resources for Parents of Troubled Teens
This website provides a number of resources on the developmental problems of adolescence, such as depression, substance abuse, and school failure.
http://www.4troubledteens.com/parent-resources.html

The Identity Development of Multiracial Youth
This link presents an article on the unique challenges that biracial and multiracial adolescents have in their quest to develop an identity.
http://www.ericfacility.net/ericdigests/ed425248.html

Adolescence: Change and Continuity
This link examines a number of issues related to adolescent identity development and self-esteem.
http://inside.bard.edu/academic/specialproj/darling/adid2.htm

Segment 17
Friendship and Popularity: Mari and Sarah, Age 13

In this segment, Mari and Sarah discuss the meaning and importance of friendship and popularity. The two best friends met at school and soon discovered that they had similar interests and personalities. Sarah illustrates how adolescents regard intimacy and loyalty as important ingredients of friendship, as she talks about how lies, dishonesty, and lack of communication can destroy a friendship. Next, Mari and Sarah give their perspective on sex differences in friendship. Finally, the girls discuss cliques, crowds, and their perceptions of what makes people popular or unpopular. Notice how they mention various influences on clique and crowd membership, such as culture, parenting practices, and personality traits.

For Discussion

1. Review the video segment, *Second Graders Discuss Friendship.* How do characteristics of adolescent friendships differ from those of younger children? Use examples from both video clips to explain your answer. (Chapter 16, pp. 608-609)

_____
_____
_____
_____
_____
_____
_____

2. How do Mari and Sarah explain sex differences in friendships? According to your text, why do these differences exist? (Chapter 16, p. 609)

A._____
_____
_____

B._____
_____
_____
_____

3. According to Mari and Sarah, how important is it to fit in with peers? Does the desire to fit in change with age? Explain. (Chapter 16, p. 607; 610)

A._____
_____

B._____
_____
_____
_____

4. What are some benefits of adolescent friendships? Can you think of others not listed in your text? (Chapter 16, pp. 609-610)

A._____

_____

_____

B._____

_____

_____

Multiple Choice Questions

1. Sarah and Mari suggested that many friendships develop from similarities between two people. Some specific similarities they identified were sex and ethnicity. Another similarity presented in your textbook is
    A. athletic ability.
    B. involvement in extracurricular activities.
    C. physical appearance.
    D. identity status.

2. Adolescent friendship is
    A. relatively unstable.
    B. related to peer status.
    C. less important in adolescence than in early or middle childhood.
    D. relatively stable.

3. The intimacy of boys' friendships is related to
    A. peer status.
    B. gender identity.
    C. dating relationships.
    D. family experiences.

4. Emotional closeness in adolescent friendship is
    A. just as important to boys as it is to girls.
    B. especially important in mixed-sex friendships.
    C. more common between girls than between boys.
    D. especially important for younger boys.

5. According to your text, many adolescent peer-group values are
    A. extensions of values acquired at home.
    B. unrelated to family values.
    C. derived from experiences with teachers.
    D. nearly identical to values held in middle childhood.

Web Links

Gender Differences in Adolescent Friendships

This link provides a review of research on gender differences in adolescent friendships, including the role of teasing.
http://inside.bard.edu/academic/specialproj/darling/bullying/group11/intimacy.html

Adolescent Friendships as Academic Resources

Using findings from the National Longitudinal Study of Adolescent Health, this article examines the relationship between adolescent friendship and positive adjustment and how friendship is influenced social structure and institutional context.
http://caliber.ucpress.net

Adolescence and Peer Pressure

This website, sponsored by the University of Nebraska, features an article on peer pressure, including strategies to help adolescents resist peer pressure.
http://ianrpubs.unl.edu/family/nf211.htm

Teen Popularity: Are You Helping or Hurting Your Child?

This link presents a quiz for parents that assesses their involvement in their teenagers' social life.
http://quiz.ivillage.com/parentsoup/tests/popular.htm?arrivalSA=1&cobrandRef=0&arrival_freqCap=1&pba=adid=11377117

Segment 18
Dating: Mike, 18 years and Haley, 17 years

In this segment, Mike and Haley describe their dating relationship, including how they first met, why they were attracted to one another, and future plans. Although Mike and Haley had previous dating experience, this relationship marked the first serious commitment for each of them. They also explain how they plan to make their relationship work while attending separate colleges.

For Discussion

1. What qualities were Mike and Haley initially attracted to in one another? Have these qualities changed over time? Explain, using examples from your text. (Chapter 16, pp. 611-612)

A._____

_____

_____

B._____

_____

_____

2. How does Mike and Haley's relationship differ from the dating relationships of younger adolescents? Based on their discussion, do you think their relationship will last as they make the transition to college? Why or why not? (Chapter 16, pp. 611-612)

A._____

_____

_____

B._____

_____

_____

3. Cite ways that adolescent friendships lay the groundwork for romantic relationships. (Chapter 16, pp. 608-612)

_____

_____

_____

_____

4. Cite the benefits of adolescent dating. How do dating experiences in adolescence influence romantic relationships in adulthood? (Chapter 16, pp. 611-612)

A._____

_____

_____

_____

B._____

_____

_____

5. Return to Chapter 7 and review research on attachment. Explain how early relationships with parents and caregivers contribute to romantic relationships in adolescence. (Chapter 16, pp. 611-612)

_____

_____

_____

_____

_____

_____

_____

Multiple Choice Questions

1. Which of the following statements about adolescent dating is TRUE?
    A. Older adolescents date primarily for superficial reasons.
    B. Both younger and older adolescents date primarily for superficial reasons.
    C. Early adolescents date primarily for superficial reasons.
    D. The achievement of intimacy in young adolescents' dating relationships is much greater than intimacy in friendships.

2. Research suggests that
    A. most adolescent dating experiences are shallow and stereotyped.
    B. experiences with parents contribute to the quality of adolescent dating relationships.
    C. Asian adolescents begin dating earlier than their Western counterparts.
    D. homosexual and heterosexual adolescents have similar dating experiences.

3. Early, frequent dating is related to
    A. drug use, delinquency, and poor academic achievement.
    B. greater social maturity.
    C. advanced moral reasoning.
    D. high self-esteem.

4. According to research presented in the text, because Mike and Haley were ready for greater psychological intimacy, they looked
    A. to one another as more of a friend than a romantic partner.
    B. for someone who could offer companionship, affection, and social support.
    C. for someone to marry.
    D. for a partner who would get along well with their families.

5. As long as it does not begin too soon, adolescent dating
    A. contributes to popularity and social status.
    B. remains superficial but helps build self-esteem.
    C. contributes to later age of first marriage.
    D. provides lessons in cooperation, etiquette, and dealing with people in a wide range of situations.

Web Links

Attachment Style Questionnaire: Experiences in Close Relationships-Revised
>This link takes you to an attachment style questionnaire that permits you to assess the quality of your close relationship. The questionnaire takes approximately 10 minutes to complete.
>http://www.web-research-design.net/cgi-bin/crq/crq.pl

Adolescent Dating
>This website provides a number of resources on adolescent dating, including fact sheets, articles, and educational programs.
>http://www.aces.edu/teens/parenteen/links/dating/dating.htm

Dating Violence Among Adolescents
>This fact sheet provides information about dating violence, including the importance of prevention programs.
>http://www.advocatesforyouth.org/publications/factsheet/fsdating.htm

WebMD Health: Survey Links Teen Dating to Drug Use
>This article presents information on the link between early teen dating, sexual activity, and substance abuse.
>http://my.webmd.com/content/article/93/102075.htm?action=related_link

EMERGING ADULTHOOD

PARTICIPANTS

Participant	Age	To identify on video, look for...
Casey	22 years	Red sweatshirt
Elizabeth	24 years	Blue sleeveless shirt
Joel	25 years	Red shirt

Segment 19

Emerging Adulthood: Elizabeth, 24 years, and Joel, 25 years

Elizabeth and Joel are recent college graduates who work as teachers of young children. As they consider whether they have truly reached adulthood, notice how they feel more mature and capable than they did as adolescents but still have not completely assumed adult responsibilities. Elizabeth and Joel also discuss their identity development, religious beliefs, and future plans.

For Discussion

1. Have you fully reached adulthood, or do you identify with the experiences of these young people? If you have not yet reached adulthood, how will you know when you reach this milestone? (Chapter 17, pp. 630-631)

A._____

_____

B._____

_____

_____

2. According to Erikson (Chapter 1, pp. 16-17), intimacy is a major task of these years. What emphasis do Elizabeth and Joel place on intimacy and establishing a lasting romantic relationship? Explain. (Chapter 17, p. 633)

A._____

_____

B._____

_____

_____

3. What role has religion played in the lives of Elizabeth and Joel? How do religiosity and spirituality change in emerging adulthood? (Chapter 17, pp. 636-637)

A._____

_____

_____

B._____

_____

_____

4. What makes emerging adulthood a particularly stressful time of life? (Chapter 17, p. 637)

_____

_____

_____

_____

5. What are some benefits of a prolonged transition to adulthood? Are there any disadvantages? Explain, using research from your text. (Chapter 17, pp. 630-636)

A._____

_____

_____

B._____

_____

_____

Multiple Choice Questions

1. Which of the following has contributed to emerging adulthood?
   A. a shortened period of adolescence
   B. dramatic gains in life expectancy in developing countries
   C. dramatic gains in life expectancy in prosperous nations
   D. early entry into the workforce

2. For many low-SES young people, emerging adulthood
   A. is limited or nonexistent.
   B. provides an escape from poverty.
   C. extends to a later age than for higher-SES young people.
   D. leads to a higher rate of high school graduation.

3. According to your text, which of the following will contribute to the quality of Elizabeth and Joel's romantic relationships?
   A. career goals
   B. their ability to balance work and family
   C. political commitments
   D. characteristics of their partners and current life conditions

4. In the video, Elizabeth and Joel comment on religion and spirituality. According to your text, emerging adults
    A. with authoritarian parents are more likely to hold religious or spiritual beliefs similar to those of their parents.
    B. with authoritative parents are more likely to hold religious or spiritual beliefs similar to those of their parents.
    C. usually attend some sort of religious service on a weekly basis.
    D. resent being asked about religiosity and spirituality.

5. Compared to older people, emerging adults
    A. are more likely to be involved in organizations devoted to specific issues of concern to them.
    B. are less likely to be involved in organizations devoted to specific issues of concern to them.
    C. have very little interest in civic or political activities.
    D. are more optimistic about the conventional political process.

Web Links

Making a Successful Transition from College to Career
This article identifies what the authors call the "eight critical issues" facing students as they make the transition from college to work, including suggestions for navigating challenges that may arise.
http://www.quintcareers.com/college-to-career.html

The Longer Road to Adulthood
This article provides an overview of emerging adulthood, including the experiences of young adults in industrialized versus developing countries.
http://www.csmonitor.com/2002/1218/p14s01-lifp.html

National Study of Youth and Religion
This website presents information on religious, civic, and political involvement. While many of the resources focus on adolescents, it also includes information relevant emerging adulthood.
http://www.youthandreligion.org/resources/ref_civic.html

Some Reflections on Post-Formal Thought
This article presents an overview of postformal thought, including its role in cognitive development and some of the controversies surrounding it.
http://www.piaget.org/GE/2001/GE-29-3.html#item2

Segment 20
Identity, Dreams, and Friendships: Casey, 22 years

Casey discusses the development of her identity, people who have influenced it, and her dreams for the future. As she describes her goals, notice how she incorporates aspects of her identity into her future plans. For instance, Casey has aspirations to establish a career prior to starting a family. As a result, she has decided to go to graduate school and enter the field of gerontology before having a family. Casey also discusses the importance of lasting friendships as she faces the challenges of emerging adulthood.

For Discussion

1. What factors have contributed to Casey's identity development? Are these factors consistent with research presented in the text? Explain. (Chapter 17, pp. 633-635)

A._____

_____

_____

B._____

_____

_____

2. What dreams does Casey mention? Are her dreams consistent with research presented in the text? Explain. (Chapter 17, pp. 634-635)

A._____

_____

B._____

_____

_____

3. Who are the mentors that are helping Casey realize her dreams? Why is having a mentor so important? (Chapter 17, pp. 634-635)

A._____

_____

B._____

_____

_____

4. Explain the obstacles to success that women may experience as they enter college and the workforce. Has Casey experienced any of these obstacles? What factors can help her overcome these obstacles? (Chapter 17, pp. 634-635)

A._____

_____

_____

B._____

_____

_____

C._____

_____

_____

5. Casey mentions the importance of her current friendships. How does the social support of good friends foster resilience in emerging adulthood? (Chapter 17, pp. 637-638)

_____

_____

_____

_____

_____

Multiple Choice Questions

1. To help realize their dream, young people
    A. typically look to their parents for help.
    B. focus on long-term goals, such as marriage and family.
    C. generally form a relationship with a mentor.
    D. generally consult a vocational counselor.

2. Identity achievement in the vocational realm is
    A. equally challenging for men and women.
    B. more challenging for women than for men.
    C. more challenging for men than for women.
    D. rarely established until young people officially transition to adulthood.

3. According to your text, which of the following is likely to promote Casey's career success?
    A. getting married in the next few years
    B. a more traditional dream
    C. frequent interaction with faculty and professors in her chosen field
    D. finding a male mentor

4. According to your text, identity changes in which of the following three areas during emerging adulthood?
    A. love, work, and worldviews
    B. cognition, social development, and worldviews
    C. morality, family, and work
    D. friendship, love, and work

Web Links

Career Coach: Interest Inventory

This link takes you to a free online Interest Inventory, which matches your interests with various career choices.

http://www.thebeehive.org/jobs/careercoach/imagine/profiler/default.asp

Learning From the Wisdom of Mentors

This website provides information on mentors, including characteristics of a good mentor and suggestions for finding a suitable mentor.

http://ilearn.senecac.on.ca/careers/experience/mentors.html

Cohabitation and Marital Success

This article, which was published in *USA Today*, summarizes some the research findings from the *National Marriage Project* at Rutgers University on the relationship between cohabitation and marital success.

http://www.usatoday.com/news/opinion/columnists/lovemarriage/love4.htm

New York State Project for Nontraditional Employment and Training

This website provides information on nontraditional careers for men and women, including tips for educators on how to decrease gender barriers.

http://www.albany.edu/nontraditionalcareers/net/L2careerNTO.htm

NOTES

NOTES

NOTES

NOTES

NOTES

NOTES

NOTES

NOTES

NOTES

NOTES